Sharing Mathematics with Parents

Planning School-Based Events

The Mathematical Association and Stanley Thornes (Publishers) Ltd

First published in 1987 by:
Stanley Thornes (Publishers) Ltd
Old Station Drive
Leckhampton
CHELTENHAM GL53 0DN
England

British Library Cataloguing in Publication Data

Sharing maths with parents.
    1.   Mathematics—Study and teaching—
Great Britain   2. Parent-teacher
relationships—Great Britain
   I.   Mathematical Association, *Teaching*
Committee
510′.7′1041   QA14.G7

ISBN 0-85950-695-9

Typeset by Tech-Set, Gateshead, Tyne & Wear
in 10/12 Souvenir Light
Printed and bound in Great Britain at The Bath Press, Avon

Contents

v

Acknowledgements

We should like to thank all those teachers, pupils, parents and advisers who took both the time and the trouble to write about mathematical events in which they had taken part, and to tell us about plans for future events. We are also grateful to the *Haverhill Echo* and the following schools for permission to use photographs:

Coleford Junior High School, Hull
Dorchester Junior High School, Hull
Four Dwellings School, Birmingham
Hodge Hill School, Birmingham
St Andrew's CE Junior High School, Hull
St Felix RC Primary School, Haverhill
Stutton Primary School, Ipswich
Tilbury Primary School, Hull
Westfield County Primary School, Haverhill
Wyke Junior High School, Hull

We would also like to thank:

The *Haverhill Echo* for the cover photograph, B Clementson, Manor Road, Haverhill for the bottom photograph on p. 20, and Humberside County Council for permission to reproduce the crossword on p. 70, from *Calculators in Class*.

Sharing Mathematics with Parents was written in 1984/86 by a sub-committee of the Teaching Committee of the Mathematical Association. The members of this committee were:

Jenny Cheetham	Redden Court School, Romford, Essex
Janet Duffin	Department of Education, Hull University
Ken Gregory	Four Dwellings School, Birmingham
Hazel Kitchener	Westfield CP, Haverhill, Suffolk
Harriet Marland (chair)	Hallgate JS, Cottingham, N Humberside
Laurie Rousham	Stutton CE CP, Ipswich, Suffolk

Introduction

SETTING THE SCENE: A CASE FOR PARENTAL INVOLVEMENT

Since the publication of the Plowden Report (*Children and their Primary Schools,* 1967), there has been an increasing awareness of the effect of parental attitudes on learning. The effects of this awareness have permeated education and resulted in increased parental involvement at all levels. Parents now exercise greater choice in selecting schools and can further influence the ethos and organisation of a school through involvement with the Parents' Association and the Governing Body, as well as by direct interaction with teachers and pupils. The government document *Better Schools* (1985) reinforces the need for education to be seen as a shared task for schools and parents. It emphasises the importance of a shared commitment, but warns that there may be deep seated obstacles resulting from parents' attitudes to schooling based on their own past experiences. We believe that the recognition that benefits can be two-way is crucial to the forging of productive interaction and partnership. Parents have as much to offer to schools as do schools to parents.

Unfortunately there are some particular problems associated with parental involvement in school mathematics. The Cockcroft Report (*Mathematics Counts,* 1982) on the teaching of mathematics in schools raises this issue. It points out that many adults fear and dislike mathematics, harbouring unhappy recollections of their own school lessons and perhaps passing on their own feelings of insecurity to their children. Moreover, the shame attached to an inability to read is not associated with a similar underachievement in mathematics. This suggests that the objective of a positive attitude towards learning mathematics, seen as so important by the writers of both the Cockcroft Report and the 1985 HMI document *Mathematics from 5 to 16,* may be almost impossible to achieve without parental cooperation.

AMBIVALENT ATTITUDES

It seems as if parents cannot win: those who were themselves successful at mathematics in school may not see the need for change from the pen and paper exercises at which they excelled; yet those who were *not* successful may be even more reluctant to appreciate changes in the mathematics curriculum!

Despite a distrust of school mathematics, parents are often extremely anxious for their children to show success in this area. A qualification in

1

mathematics is still sometimes seen as a panacea for the uncertainties of the employment market and for coping with the enormous technological changes which are taking place. Even five-year-olds can feel under pressure from their parents to do 'proper sums'. Thus it should not be so surprising that a recent survey in a national newspaper claimed that only 20 per cent of the sample admitted liking mathematics while 82 per cent believed it to be the single most important subject taught in school!

Schools are uniquely placed to help resolve this paradox by extending to parents the opportunity to confront their anxieties both about mathematics and about the way in which it is taught. Most schools include in their calendar an 'open' day or evening for parents. Such occasions vary in their format from school to school, but the general aim is usually to display the work of the school and to designate some time for discussing the progress of individual pupils. Only rarely is there much discussion of curricular issues, yet, since these events are familiar to all of us, they could easily be developed so as to increase the opportunities for discussion of the mathematics curriculum. Section 1 of this book suggests ways to extend and adapt 'open days' in order to facilitate such discussion, and also outlines a wider variety of 'mathematical events' which seek to involve parents in doing more mathematics themselves.

Inevitably, as with all new ventures, problems may arise. Parents may be loath to join in specifically mathematical activities; pupils may be overexuberant or insufficiently prepared for the tasks they undertake; teachers may be diffident about teaching with parents present. But, as with so much of what we teach, the process is at least as important as the product and we should not expect '10 out of 10' all the time! Many of the stories told by parents, pupils and teachers in Section 1 demonstrate that, even though events are seldom perfect, the mutual confidence of all three parties involved continues to grow.

MATHEMATICAL EVENTS MUST PROLIFERATE!

Many situations within a school can provide an initial impetus for parental involvement. These can arise from a 'whole-school policy' or from the mathematics department alone.

The introduction of a new mathematics scheme or course provides an opportunity to introduce parents to the material and methods involved. Similarly the increasing use of calculators and computers could provide a starting point. The introduction of the GCSE provides another valuable motive for contact, especially since it involves new forms of assessment. In addition to these, the annual arrival of a new intake of children gives a regular opportunity to reach another set of parents and might even start a tradition of parental involvement in mathematics within the school which could stretch into the years ahead.

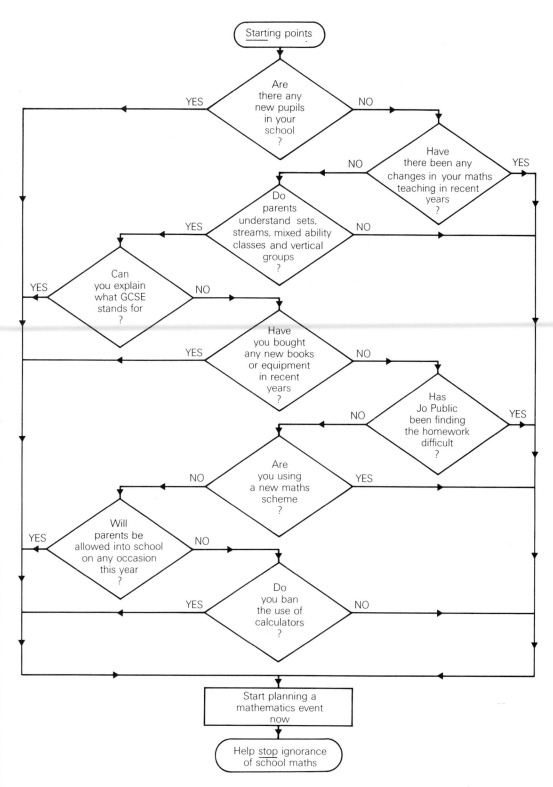

Plan a mathematics event!

MAINTAINING THE MOMENTUM

Once parents are intrigued by the mathematics of the school, other developments become possible. Here are a few examples:

- A computer club open to both parents and children can help to cement common interests.

- A stall in school selling mathematical books, games and puzzles can increase the number of mathematical activities used at home.

- Sessions for parents, together with children, to use mathematical apparatus in practical activities can open up discussion and lead to the development of a common vocabulary.

- Occasional mathematical trails, circuses or other diversions can be arranged for weekend participation.

- Telephone help-lines can provide parents and pupils alike with an opportunity to discuss any mathematical uncertainties they may have, even when the school is closed.

SECTION 1 **Involving Parents**

This section begins with two diagrams illustrating a range of events through which any school can increase parents' awareness of mathematics. Each type of event is then described in greater detail. The Scope sections indicate some of the possible advantages and disadvantages of advertising mathematics in each of these ways. Methods of organisation and a few helpful tips are also included. In the sections entitled How it Worked, parents, pupils and teachers recall mathematical events in which they themselves took part.

1 An Overview

Presenting Mathematics to Parents

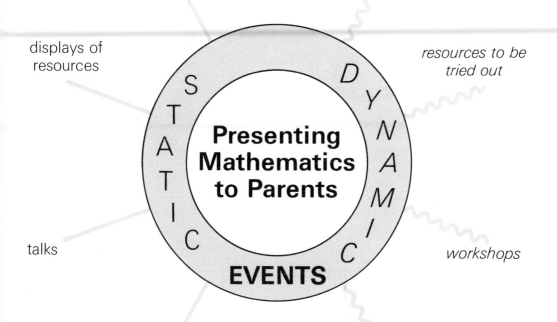

displays of work

pupils at work

displays of resources

resources to be tried out

Presenting Mathematics to Parents

talks

workshops

EVENTS

stalls selling books and games

mathematical games and entertainments

Parents in Partnership

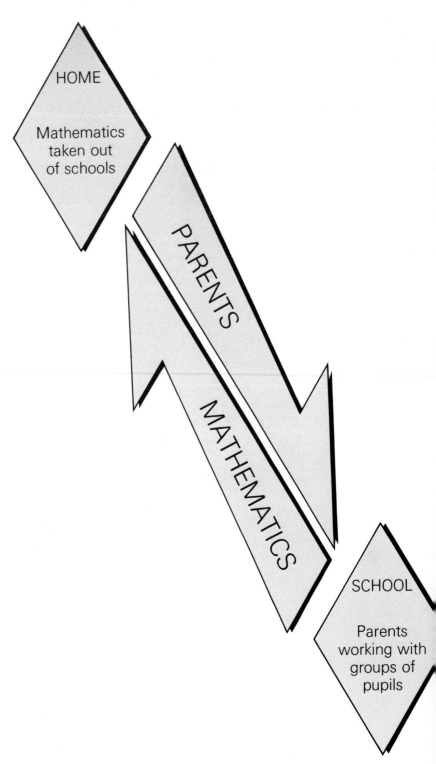

2 Displays of Work

Scope

- Suitable for all occasions when the school is open to parents, e.g. open days, parents' evenings, concerts, etc.

- Can be made to fit in with a whole school theme, e.g. 'Transport'.

- Could highlight a particular area of the mathematics curriculum, e.g. 'Mathematics Around Us', 'The Use of Calculators', etc.

ADVANTAGES	DISADVANTAGES
Does not need to be supervised, so teachers are free to talk with parents.	*Can only show the product of mathematics lessons, not the process of mathematical thinking.*
Can include work from every pupil.	*Any display takes a long time to prepare.*
Can be viewed over a period of time and on a number of separate occasions.	*Some visitors may judge the display on fairly superficial qualities.*

A display of work should have a purpose beyond that of filling in blank spaces on the walls! Such a purpose might be: 'to show the variety of mathematics covered by one year group'; 'to show how one topic is developed throughout the school and across the ability levels'; 'to illustrate the mathematics used in all subjects'; 'to indicate how the teaching of the school reflects the precepts of the Cockroft Report'; 'to suggest how parents can use activities out of school to help pupils use and enjoy mathematics' etc., etc. The possibilities are endless. It is usually best to decide the theme and the purpose of the display well in advance. This allows you to be more critical, although not necessarily more selective, in accumulating examples that may be included. It also allows you, at an early stage, to delegate some of the responsibility for collecting materials. If you ask each teacher to save nice examples of mathematics from their groups you are unlikely to get much at all. If you ask for a sample of each type of graph constructed, or for a display measuring 1.50 m by 0.7 m of the mathematical aspects of the term's topic work, you should get something (or at least the opportunity to grumble if you don't!). It will also help everyone if you make clear from the start the standard of work you are looking for: do you want *all* the work on one aspect; each child's individual best work; mathematically sound and correct work only; fair copies or work cut out from exercise books?

You also need plenty of time to collect materials. If you are concentrating on a topic-related display, a term may be adequate but, if you are illustrating the full breadth of the work you cover, you need to start collecting things a year in advance. In fact it may be wise just to become a perpetual hoarder of mathematics work since it is often unrealistic to expect a full year's notice of forthcoming events.

Delegation and forethought are vital to producing a successful display. It also helps to become something of a thief, or at least an entrepreneur. Make sure you notice the work on other people's blackboards and walls and use it whenever you can. Is there any art work using symmetry, pattern-making, proportion, measurement or enlargement? Are graphs and tables being constructed and used in physics, geography or home economics? Do blackboard notes suggest that there are exciting mathematical activities going on that may not have been recorded? Once you get a name for actually wanting other people's 'irrelevant rubbish' you will find your colleagues become more willing to hand over work that they believe is better!

A display of work need not, of course, be limited to exercises on paper. Three-dimensional models, photographs or video and audio cassettes of pupils working have a place too. However, during the months that you are hoarding away all these offerings you should also be planning the best way to present the materials you have gathered. Remember that people going round the display will have only a limited time to see it, and you need to classify, annotate and display the mathematics as carefully as any museum would exhibit the latest archaeological finds of a little-known human civilisation!

A few tips:
- Paper for mounting and double-mounting A4 and A5 sheets can be obtained from some suppliers. Alternatively you could pre-cut your own mounting paper to standard widths, and trim them to the required length as you mount each sample. Some work, e.g. standard exercises or homework sheets, might look pretentious if double-mounted, but can stand out well if fixed directly on to a striking background.

- The backing can be made to reflect the topic of the work too. For example, 2-D geometry work could be set against a backing of large polygons; 3-D work in a 3-D setting using a stack of odd pieces of school furniture arranged like a sculpture or draped with a cloth; solutions of a problem could be mounted against a pictorial representation of the problem situation; topic related examples, such as the mathematics of the train, could be mounted on a relevant silhouette.

- Large areas of wall or window can be covered quickly with work which has already been mounted on to rolls of frieze paper, wallpaper or even paper ribbons. (The backing paper is secured at the last moment at ceiling and skirting levels.)

- Notices can be written on the reverse side of paper printed with 1 cm or 2 cm squares. The outlines of the squares serve to guide the writing but become invisible when the notice is set against a dark background.

How it Worked:

USING THE HALL DURING A MATHEMATICS EVENING

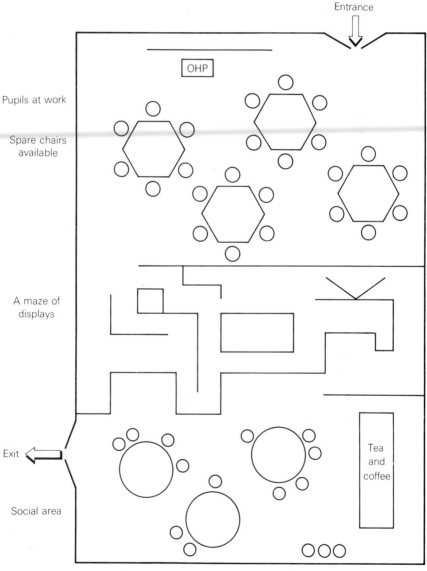

At Hodge Hill School, Birmingham, they used a maze of displays as a transition from a demonstration lesson to a social area

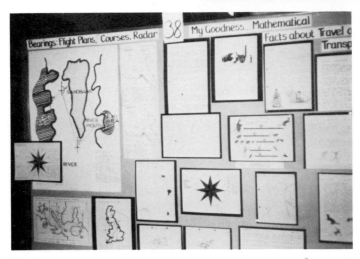

Displays

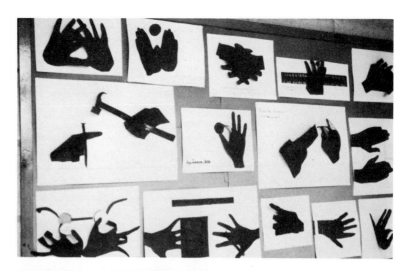

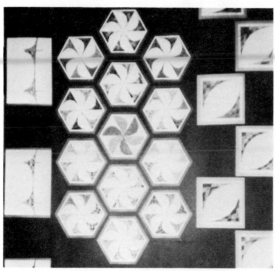

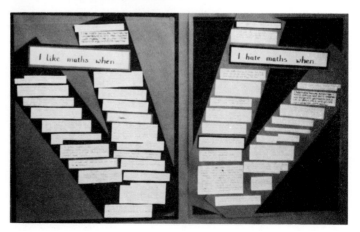

Displays – of mathematics?

13

3   Pupils at Work

Scope

- Suitable for general open days or for a 'mathematics spectacular.'

- Groups could demonstrate work in particular areas such as problem-solving or practical measurement.

- A complete lesson could be worked or different styles of teaching could be highlighted.

- Pupils could instruct parents.

- If every teacher teaches mathematics, the whole school could be involved simultaneously.

ADVANTAGES	DISADVANTAGES
Parents become more aware of the atmosphere and philosophy of the school.	*If the event is held during the school day, there will be a lot of people in a confined space.*
Parents can talk to pupils at work and pupils gain in confidence by explaining the work in progress.	*If the event is held in the evening, there may be problems in getting the required pupils to return.*
Parents may appreciate some of the changes in the mathematics curriculum.	*Parents may challenge the method or presentation of the lesson and it may be necessary to have other teachers available to explain what is happening.*

If you want to create a more dynamic atmosphere when parents visit a school to look at mathematics, the involvement of pupils is almost essential. These pupils can become actively involved in a variety of ways, and will, one hopes, transmit an interest and enthusiasm for the mathematics in which they are involved.

Being Taught

This approach supposes that a willing member of staff can be found to prepare and give a lesson to a whole class or group of pupils in front of parents. A time-scale needs to be decided for the lesson, and this will depend on both the topic and the expected flow of parents. Visitors might be invited to stay for the whole 'lesson' to see how a complete segment of the chosen topic is developed; alternatively, they could circulate freely as the lesson progressed over the period of perhaps an hour. Certainly a larger than average room would be required if a full class of pupils was present; whereas a teacher-led group activity could easily take place in a corner of a room with displays all around.

Demonstrating Mathematical Activities

In this approach pupils are used more as the 'teachers' or 'instructors' of parents. They could show how a wide variety of equipment, games and other activities are used to convey, reinforce and develop mathematical concepts and skills. With good briefing and a trial run beforehand, they could be asked to involve interested parents and explain the objectives of the activity. The number of individual items presented in this way would depend very largely on the availability of space and suitable pupils.

Collecting Information

For the purpose of teaching statistics, graphwork and the analysis of data, there is always a need for practice in information gathering. A steady supply of eager parents for an hour or so would seem to provide an irresistible source of interesting data just waiting to be 'captured'. With appropriate classroom preparation, pupils could measure and observe visiting parents thus collecting real data to be used as the subject of further work in mathematics lessons. Graphs can be drawn, calculations made and trends and patterns observed. In some cases it might be desirable to display the data immediately. For example, younger pupils could create a block graph of birth months using standard size 'birthday cards'.

Another useful exercise is to try out questionnaires constructed in class. These need not be long, but they would give more meaning to the problems involved in the preparation of questionnaires as well as the analysis of the data accumulated.

A few tips:
- Other teachers may have the same idea, and so it would be wise to 'book' the required pupils early – bribery may be necessary!

- You must be prepared to limit your activities to whatever you feel you can supervise, and should not risk overwhelming parents or distracting them from viewing other parts of the presentation.

- It is obviously essential to have all the necessary equipment available and checked.

- The detailed briefing of pupils beforehand will make for a more confident realisation of the objectives of the whole event. Other members of staff, including dinner supervisors or cleaners, make valuable 'guinea pigs' for a trial run before the event.

- If an evening event is planned, it might be possible to send pupils home for the afternoon beforehand.

How it Worked:

i BACK TO SCHOOL FOR MUMS AND DADS

We aimed to give parents a greater understanding of how their children approached mathematics. All the classes were involved for two separate half days – including the nursery. Parents were free to wander around the school and they were encouraged to talk to the children and become involved with various activities. A handout was provided giving a brief outline of the activities of each class. In this way parents saw the progression of mathematics throughout the school and learned the value of counting action rhymes, sorting, etc.

We stressed to all parents that language development through maths was a priority of our total approach, and we were able to explain to them how they could extend this at home with maths activities round the house, out shopping, travelling, etc.

The children, feeling confident and relaxed in their own environment, seized the opportunity to turn the tables on their parents. Comments and feedback from parents were very encouraging. They realised that we were not leading the children by the hand through the various mathematical experiences, but rather equipping them with whatever is necessary for them to go out and explore the wider world with confidence and understanding. Parents were delighted with all the structural apparatus and they began to see it as a valuable aid to learning rather than a plaything. They commented on how much fun the children obviously got out of learning – often quite the reverse of their own past experiences.

Since the event, many parents have asked if they might join in the maths activities during the school day. We are, of course, very happy with this extra help.

J Bestwick (St Felix RC Primary School, Suffolk)

ii PARENTS OBSERVING A LESSON

A lesson with a group of nine- and ten-year-olds constructing 3-D shapes from card was observed by parents. One parent said, 'Oh, he'll do that sort of maths all day,' implying that, because it was of a practical nature, it wasn't proper maths at all. Others were pleased. They thought the work was a challenge to their children and were amazed at the patience and dexterity shown. One boy bragged that his father would not be able to do it – and his father had to agree.

In another group, pupils were working out areas using a variety of methods. Some parents were impatient: knowing the rules of area themselves they wanted to tell their own children straightaway. They saw the counting activities as just a waste of time and I had to explain their relevance.

Many parents said that the maths demonstrated was more fun than the maths they had been used to.

Sue Steer (St Andrew's CE JHS, Hull)

iii A PUPIL'S-EYE VIEW

When Miss asked would I like to do this maths on the open evening I said 'Yes'. Then she said I would have to teach mothers and fathers on that night and I was afraid I would not do it right. When I arrived I felt cold inside of me, but anyway I just asked the first mother if she would like to have a go. She looked puzzled at first and I was nervous, but I showed her what to do and it was alright after that. Later Miss said I had taught her teacher from college to make shapes and we laughed. It was great, I would like to do it again.

Michelle Harker (aged 11)

(Michelle was working on symmetry puzzles with plastic shapes and a flexible mirror.)

iv A LIVE LESSON

Some time ago I was approached by my Head of Department and asked to make a special contribution to our forthcoming open evening. This contribution was to take the form of a 'live lesson' so that prospective parents, for whom the evening was being planned, could gain some insight into the teaching of mathematics at our school.

My initial reaction to this request was that, try as I might, certain factors would render it impossible to recreate a typical lesson. For example, the format of the evening was such that I was to be stationed with my 'class' in a different room from my usual one. Groups of parents would then 'visit' us at different times to see how the lesson was progressing. Since the evening was scheduled to last almost one and a half hours, this meant that my pupils and I would, in effect, be staging a continuous performance for that duration. Just think . . . how many lessons actually last that long without a break?

Also, since the activities were to take place in the evening, and our Department had jointly decided that I should work with a group of first-year pupils, I envisaged problems in finding 'volunteers'. As it happened, I managed to find a small group of eight individuals who were more than willing to help out, and whose parents were agreeable to them participating in the event. Again, how many of us are fortunate enough to encounter classes of eight in the general course of our teaching?

Having established who I would be teaching, my next job was to decide what I would teach. After discussing this matter with my colleagues it was decided that I should develop a lesson based on Euler's Law. This topic would allow plenty of scope for discussion as well as work of both a practical and written nature. We felt that, through this topic, it would be possible to demonstrate some of the different teaching methods used in the Department.

Since the actual location of the lesson was to be a science laboratory, the pupils were seated around one large bench. This proved to be ideal for our purposes because throughout the lesson everyone could see clearly what was going on. It also meant that the pupils were less shy about joining in any discussion than, I feel, they would have been had they been sitting in rigid rows.

Thus, armed with various packages as real examples of solids in everyday use, and a set of perspex demonstration solids, I proceeded to develop the necessary language and eventually the group derived Euler's Law. What pleased me was that on a few occasions the visitors actually became involved in the lesson. The children became most excited as they saw a pattern emerging, and seemed only too happy to share their discoveries with the adults.

Our main aim had been to give parents some idea of our approach to the teaching of mathematics in our school, and the pupils' sheer delight at discovering Euler's Law for themselves, and their obvious enjoyment of the lesson, must surely have left the visitors with a favourable impression.

Pat Armitage (Four Dwellings Secondary, Birmingham)

Lessons observed

19

Parents learning – pupils teaching

4 Displays of Resources

Scope
- Suitable for any time when parents are in the school.
- New acquisitions and gifts from the Parents' Association could be acknowledged.

ADVANTAGES	DISADVANTAGES
Parents can see the variety of resources used.	*Does not explain how or why the resources are used and this can cause misunderstanding.*
Parents can see how money is spent.	*Needs to be supervised – or out of reach!*

All schools have a variety of resources for the teaching of mathematics which could be displayed. These items may range from workcards and textbooks to practical equipment for measuring and surveying, and from structural apparatus for numberwork to software for the microcomputer. Merely creating a display of such resources in a public place can begin to convey to visitors the range of resources used in the teaching of mathematics, and can indicate the breadth of teaching methods used. However it is important to do more than just arrange the equipment on tables – some attempt has to be made to put the items on display into context within the mathematics curriculum. This could be done with explanatory notes; by including samples of pupils' work; through a tape-recorded message; or by having pupils and teachers on hand to answer questions. (It may also be appropriate in the display to indicate the cost of buying some of the items – especially if the Parents' Association has supported the purchase, or is planning to fund a particular project.)

5 Resources to be Tried Out

Scope
- Suitable for open days or mathematical events.
- Resources can be shown alongside the mathematics generated from them.

ADVANTAGES	DISADVANTAGES
Parents can discover how the resources aid understanding.	*Needs to be supervised by staff and/or pupils.*
Pupil involvement with parents can increase the confidence of both parties.	*Parents may dispute the educational value of the resources, so carefully chosen activities and well-briefed supervisors are essential.*
	Valuable activities may be time-consuming.

Much of the equipment that could be displayed may lend itself to being handled and actually used by parents. Thus notices might invite parents to try the equipment as if they were pupils. A written explanation of how to proceed, or samples of pupils' workcards may be sufficient to tempt some parents to 'have a go'. However, here would be an excellent opportunity to use pupils as instructors, challenging parents to play mathematical games, solve puzzles and use apparatus to arrive at mathematical conclusions. For the pupils, the exercise of having to provide explanations would be most valuable, but it would be a good idea to have a member of staff available to oversee the operation and answer any more awkward questions.

How it Worked:

PUPILS' REPORT

Our last open evening was good as some of us could help by doing games and things like we do in lessons. Our group was working with calculators. We showed the parents what we do in class. It was sometimes very difficult to explain it right but mostly we managed. We asked them to do a crossword with us. Some parents did it, some just passed on and could not care less but mostly they asked if they could take one home for their children – so we let them.

Rebecca Jones (aged 10) with **Mark Brady** and **Stephen Allenby** (aged 12)

Calculators – on display and in use

6

Talks

Scope

- Can be used to introduce parents to the teaching and organisation of mathematics in the school, or to explain changes in the schemes and syllabuses in use.

- Could be used to develop mathematical ideas or as a forum for debate on topical issues.

- Different times of day will suit different audiences.

ADVANTAGES	DISADVANTAGES
Can help to put the school's mathematics into a wider context.	Allows only limited dialogue between parents and teachers.
An outside speaker can be seen to reinforce the school's philosophy from a position of authority.	Parents may be less willing to attend events which do not seem to concern their children directly.
Provides a forum for the discussion of topical, and even controversial, issues.	

A good, sensitive speaker may inform, intrigue and even inspire the listeners. An inept speaker may not only bore the audience but may also provide a generous forum for the most antagonistic of parents to voice their opinions! As the organiser, you need to be able to influence the atmosphere and keep it positive.

The topic and the speaker should be chosen with care so as to involve parents rather than alienate them. You know the parents of your pupils best and in choosing both the speaker and the time for the talk you will need to consider what sort of person is likely to come. For example:

1 Will you have a number of confident and outspoken people who may be entrenched in the 'back to basics' rut, and who will certainly want to come in and argue about the newfangled nonsense taught nowadays – whatever the topic of the talk is?

2 Will there be many diffident parents who feel (perhaps quite wrongly) that their own mathematics is suspect and who will not feel secure enough to enter into the discussion unless coaxed?

3 Are there likely to be people whose main interests lie with other subjects and who have little sympathy for, or understanding of, the teaching of mathematics?

Giving a talk to parents demands different skills from those of teaching children or running workshops for teachers, and it would be rash to assume that a good teacher or lecturer will necessarily make a good speaker for parents attending a mathematics event at school. Obviously people you have heard yourself, or who have been recommended to you, are the safest bet. Speakers from outside could include advisers for mathematics or for the age/ability range in question; advisory teachers; lecturers; publishers; industrialists and other professionals; former pupils; etc. If, however, you are going to do the talk yourself it is worth looking at the AVA packs available (see Chapter 17 for details).

A few tips:
- Make it absolutely clear, in writing and through discussion with the speaker, what the purpose of the talk is and how long it should last.

- Inform the speaker what resources are available for AVA, and ensure that they really are available and that they work!

- Consider having a forum started by three short talks as an alternative to one long talk.

- Have a back-up team ready to answer questions and include on it at least one person who has a reputation for answering awkward or obscure questions with tact.

- If all else fails and the parents seem unresponsive, mention subtraction!

How it Worked:

TWO VIEWS OF THE SAME TALK

One View

At a previous school I became aware that I was spending a considerable amount of time explaining individually to parents what was happening in mathematics and why. I began to realise that as the numbers in the school had been steadily rising there were many new parents who had missed earlier opportunities of finding out about the school's mathematics teaching. Having identified the need, the question was what to do next: What did parents want? Would they prefer an exhibition of work, a talk or seeing the children at work? Some 'sounding out' of parents indicated that a talk on the present approach to mathematics would be the most appropriate.

The next consideration was should we, the teachers, do this or should we involve someone outside the school? If so, who? It had to be someone who knew something about the school, or knew some of the staff and would be able to communicate with parents in large or small numbers, as we had no idea how many would turn up. One of my colleagues recommended a local lecturer in teacher education and I went to see her to discuss possibilities – I felt it was important for me to meet her first.

After due consideration it was decided to arrange a meeting for parents at which she would talk generally about changes in the mathematics curriculum. This would be followed by a short talk by one or two members of staff about the teaching of mathematics within the school. An exhibition of equipment and materials would be set up in the hall.

A large proportion of parents came bringing views ranging from 'Why change things? What I learned has been good enough for me and will be for my children' to 'I couldn't do maths at school but my children enjoy it and I would like to be able to help them at home.'

At first the parents sat quite still, listening politely, but not actively involved. This changed suddenly when subtraction was mentioned, and parents were asked how they would solve a simple example. Very quickly they were involved and from then on there was no lack of opinion and comment! Another controversial point concerned the use of calculators in school.

At these two points it would have been easy to 'lose' the audience but both incidents were used to maximum effect by the speaker, and they helped to create a more relaxed atmosphere. The parents were not made to feel that their views did not matter.

At the end of the meeting some of the parents expressed an interest in coming into school for informal workshop sessions. These workshop sessions were organised by a member of staff during the school day. A number of the parents who came said that they had a greater understanding of what their children were doing and why.

These workshop sessions were a direct result of the talk to parents.

H Kitchener (Westfield CP School, Haverhill, Suffolk)

Another View

From the point of view of the receivers, and of the school perhaps, talks are included in the 'passive' or static part of the wheel of parental involvement; from the point of view of the giver of talks this may not be the case at all.

I have given several in-school talks to parents and would prefer to see them as talk/workshops rather than pure talks because, being a teacher

26

myself, I cannot operate in a vacuum of non-response. I look for and feed on the responses I get. These can be various – between talks because of different types of audience, but also within a talk in terms both of different responses from different people and a changing response as the talk progresses.

Two of the talks to parents have been evening ones with both mothers and fathers present; the other was an afternoon one with only mothers attending, in spite of the school being in an area of high unemployment. Perhaps because it was daytime, perhaps because the numbers were small, perhaps because only mothers were present, perhaps for a combination of all these reasons, the involvement of the parents was more immediate on the daytime occasion. Indeed it was most genuinely a workshop for, after only a short input from me using activity with equipment and the talk arising from it, the mothers were eager to enter into the activity themselves, asked questions and responded by seeing the significance in their own lives of what we were doing. They also contrasted it with their own memories of mathematics at school and began to feel how lucky their children were.

I should like to describe in more detail one of the two evening talks, and hope that it may be possible to abstract some general notions about the hazards and rewards of talks. The Head of the school and her teacher in charge of mathematics were both fully committed to the newer ideas in mathematics, but they had met with some objections and queries arising from parents' misgivings about methods and content.

They rightly felt that some visual support for what I would be saying was needed and, as the talk took place in the months immediately following the publication of the Cockcroft Report (1982), they had chosen some apt quotations from the report which were pinned up as a welcome framework and back-up for me as I faced this friendly, though clearly daunting, set of parents.

I never cease to feel nervous at encountering a new group whether they be students, children, teachers or (as in this case) parents, and I greatly appreciated the Head's quiet presence beside me as I rose to start my talk.

At first the parents listened quietly and without comment. My eyes scanned the listening faces and I discerned little, except that perhaps the mothers looked slightly more receptive but in a somewhat diffident way. This was not to be the case throughout the evening.

It was when I used the talk to involve the parents in thinking about their own mathematics that the evening first came alive. I asked them to think about the process of subtraction, to do a subtraction which I put on the board and to note the words they said to themselves as they did it. I then asked for volunteers to tell us all exactly what they did and said in a subtraction 'sum'. The effect was electric and forms of words like 'put it on the doorstep', 'give a ten and take one', 'borrow one and pay it back', 'five from two you can't . . .' flew about the room. Passive?

27

We identified the two principal subtraction methods and many were surprised to learn that there was any other way than the one they knew. Some were disconcerted and anxious to rush home to see how their children did it, worried because they may have inadvertently confused their children brought up on a different method. Some said, and this particularly seemed true of the mothers, that they had never understood it before – that it made sense at last. We spoke briefly of the place of language in mathematics and the need for it to be appropriate to the process. I was able to indicate how the newer methods enabled us to help children to understand processes like subtraction through the use of equipment and experience of equal additions not affecting the answer in a subtraction.

This was rewarding: for them because it illuminated a well-drilled but ill-understood process; for me because it made the mothers at least more receptive to the other ideas I wished to put forward. However, I had not entirely convinced the fathers. This came out later in their questions and comments when I ventured to suggest (my notes on the occasion show that I regretted this suggestion in 1982 after the event, but I would certainly have no such regrets now) that the arrival of calculators had largely undermined the need for children to practise assiduously the four traditional arithmetical processes of addition, subtraction, multiplication and division with increasingly large numbers extending eventually to the same thing with decimals.

After the positive effects of the investigation of subtraction, the response to calculators was disappointing and disconcerting. The fathers, and one mother, spoke of falling standards and said 'What was good enough for me . . .' and 'Calculators have made me lazy so should not be given to children'.

I countered these arguments as best I could, fearing that I might be undermining any confidence that existed between parents and teachers, that the school would regret their mistake in asking me to come and that I might have undone the good that the staff's own patient perseverance in the face of parental misgivings had so far done.

The Head was tact and diplomacy itself. She calmed me and the fathers, and suggested we break up for informal discussion with the teachers who were there to help, and to view the school's equipment.

For me, the speaker, the eruption of opposition seemed destructive at the time and I temporarily forgot the earlier positive response I had provoked. In retrospect, I think that some parents had indeed become more receptive to mathematics as a result of their experience. In retrospect too, I think I anticipated the calculator revolution and so a negative response bringing antagonisms into the open was inevitable. Now there would be even more positive backing for calculators than the Cockcroft Report then offered me.

The evening had therefore progressed through passivity to involvement and to conflict. It had brought out into the open parental prejudices and it had enabled some parents to move from a sense of confused incomprehension to the illumination of an understanding of processes rooted in their own past experience of mathematics, and through that had made them more perceptive about future possibilities.

Janet Duffin (Department of Educational Studies, Hull University)

7

Workshops

Scope
- Could be a single event or form part of a series.
- Could usefully extend the ideas raised in an earlier talk or points made by parents when viewing lessons and trying resources, etc.

ADVANTAGES	DISADVANTAGES
Parents have direct experience of learning mathematics.	*Requires meticulous organisation.*
Increases the communication between pupil, parent and teacher.	*There may be a small response initially.*
	Without a follow-up of further sessions the achievements may be limited.
	A series of workshops requires long term commitment from all those involved.

The thought of going back to school for a series of 'maths lessons' is guaranteed to turn most parents instantly into truants! However, although workshops do involve a lot of work for parents, pupils and teachers alike, they can be very rewarding too.

The starting point for the workshops is often the suggestion (voiced by parents at meetings, in private or through their children) that mathematics, for better or worse, is not what it used to be. 'I used to enjoy sums, but I can't help little Adam with his homework now'; 'Beth seems to do nothing but play in her maths lessons – when is she going to do some proper work?'; 'We could *never* use calculators when *I* was at school, you had to *really* know your numbers then!' etc. So in publicising the sessions you need to make it clear from the outset that parents will be offered an opportunity to experience the *methods* involved in the teaching of mathematics, but will not necessarily be asked to learn the topics covered by their own children.

A lot of work needs to be done in advance. You can find out approximately how many people hope to come, but you cannot expect to know their aptitude for mathematics. The range of ability in any group will probably exceed that of your most mixed-ability classes: some parents may claim to know nothing at all, while others will be delighted to find that their skills exceed yours! Either a short explanatory talk or an easy 'ice breaker' (see Section 2 for some examples) might make a good opening activity, but thereafter you will need a variety of worksheets which can be tackled at different levels so as to maintain the interest of everyone. You could keep the organisation more fluid by asking parents to move on to different work areas whenever a bell rings.

A plenary session at the end can be useful for tackling general questions, although a break for tea can provide as much opportunity for people to ask questions and maintain a more informal atmosphere.

A few tips:

- Prepare and test all worksheets well in advance.

- Have enough assistants (pupils and/or staff) to answer questions as they arise from the work. Give all helpers ample opportunity to assess and discuss the worksheets before the event.

- One member of staff should be appointed as official 'trouble-shooter' to patrol all the work areas and to deal with any difficulties which might arise. (Someone who is not usually involved in the teaching of mathematics can often be a most effective defuser of potentially explosive situations!)

- Make sure all requirements – worksheets, equipment, paper, writing materials, etc. – are available before the parents arrive, and that the work areas are tidy and comfortable.

- It is useful to hold meetings of all staff and pupils involved as soon as possible after the event, in order to plan an even better one for next time!

How it Worked:

i INTRODUCING A NEW SCHEME

We decided to set up some mathematical workshops for parents, as a follow-up to a mathematics evening held in school, since we were convinced that parents wanted to help, yet felt unable to do so because they did not fully understand the mathematics scheme themselves. Many parents had already bought the workbooks and had gone through them with their children at a faster rate than we did at school – though, of course they had not used the teachers' manual nor any of the preparatory and supplementary work for each section. This caused problems for the children who often became bored or confused, and it caused dissatisfaction amongst the parents who thought we were holding their children back.

A group of about 20 parents with children between the ages of four and eight years (including some with pre-school children) attended the workshops. I made a set of overhead projector slides which listed each section of the scheme and gave examples of the language and types of recording used. I gave a brief description of each section and how we would teach the mathematical concepts within it. I also put out a selection of practical apparatus, workcards and sheets to demonstrate each area covered, and gave the parents the opportunity to use these. We concluded each section with questions and discussion.

The parents who attended were enthusiastic – particularly when they saw the point of an exercise in the workbooks which had previously eluded them. They were very interested in looking at the display of equipment but were reluctant to take part in any practical activities. They were open-minded and motivated to discover what the scheme was all about and how it related to the mathematics which they had learned at school, often commenting that it seemed much more interesting and that their children enjoyed it. They also appreciated, and approved of, the emphasis on understanding rather than learning by rote. With one exception the workshops were attended by mothers, but perhaps this had more to do with the timing of the sessions than with parental attitudes to mathematics.

From their reactions, I felt that it had been worthwhile although the practical sessions were not a great success. (It might have been more advantageous to produce worksheets of enrichment activities which parents could follow with their children in the privacy of their own homes.) I also felt that there should have been more opportunity for parents to describe where problems and misunderstandings arose and what they wanted from the workshops. As usual more time was needed and, as the headteacher was covering my class, the time available was limited and depended on the staffing within the school. We felt that it would be very useful to run similar sessions specifically for parents of pre-school children to explain the importance and variety of early mathematical experiences in the home.

Sue Helliwell (Acre Head CP, Hull)

ii PUPILS WHO HAD HELPED

iii A PARENT WHO PARTICIPATED

I have always felt that my mathematical background was adequate. However, since my children are reaching secondary school age, I have been rather loth to offer them assistance with homework, as I had the fear that the maths and ways of teaching it had changed beyond all recognition. I was afraid of muddling them and of losing face if I did not understand what they were doing. Therefore, I was delighted to have the opportunity of 'going back to school' and discovering more about today's maths. It was nice to have youngsters present, obviously enjoying themselves and with a good grasp of the subject. The staff were helpful, in spite of not having enough time to get round to everyone as and when they might have liked. I found the evening a great success. I realised that there was probably a much narrower gap between ancient and modern mathematics than I had feared, and I have been able to discuss this with my daughter and look forward with anticipation to the next such event.

(This father prefers not to be named.)

8 Stalls Selling Books, Equipment, Software, Games, etc.

Scope
- Suitable for any occasion when the school is open to parents, including the beginning and end of the school day.

ADVANTAGES	DISADVANTAGES
Can provide an opportunity to advise parents about the suitability of equipment etc.	*Requires supervision, accounting and management.*
Can help to get more mathematical activities used in the home.	*Misunderstanding is possible over what is desirable and how to use it.*
Can be used to raise money.	

Firstly you must decide what you want to sell and how to obtain it. Local toyshops and bookshops will often provide a wide range of items on a sale or return basis, and a percentage rebate on the actual sales should be negotiable. If your event is large enough, the supplier may even run the stall for you. Larger or more specialised equipment (such as a specific model of calculator) may be ordered for resale through some major educational suppliers.

The situation of the stall is also important since people will only buy things if they have the leisure, as well as the money, to do so. Ideally the stall should be set up where both parents and children congregate and have few other distractions. The entrance hall might be suitable, or near the 'teas', or indeed anywhere there is likely to be a queue!

Since small items such as pencils are likely to be some of the most popular articles on sale, your profit margins will be small. It is therefore essential to have a foolproof trading and accounting system. A clearly visible receipt such as a coloured sticky label or a date stamp can save time and prevent errors.

If your sale of mathematics-related items is a success, you might try to persuade the school tuck-shop or bookstall to stock some of the more profitable articles thereafter.

A very different kind of stall is one in which parents are encouraged to buy items for the school. One such event, instigated by a publisher, worked as follows: a display of *desired* books was on view throughout the evening next to a bookcase (initially empty) for *acquired* books. Parents were invited to purchase a book, complete a label to say who was presenting it to the school and then add the book to the growing number in the bookcase.

A stall of any kind will need adult supervisors as well as pupil volunteers. Since teachers are likely to be busy in other areas, it may well be that here is an area in which the Parents' Association or other sympathetic parents can become instantly involved in mathematics within the school.

9 Games and Entertainments

Scope

- Suitable for any occasion when the school is open and there is time for recreational activities.

ADVANTAGES	DISADVANTAGES
Can involve parents who would be hesitant in joining other mathematical activities.	*Needs to be organised and supervised by staff and/or pupils.*
Can involve younger siblings and thus allow more parents to attend.	*The organisers must be prepared to explain the value of any activity.*
Can encourage the use of mathematical games at home.	

A room where mathematical games and entertainments are in progress can prove a great attraction for parents as well as children. It is a good idea to set up the games in the hall or room where refreshments are to be served, so that parents can watch and join in at leisure without feeling that they should be rushing on to see the 'real' mathematics.

The games can be set up and organised by pupils. They should be simple enough to be picked up quite easily by anyone who cares to join in. Mathematical versions of dominoes, snap and happy families; calculator games and card games might all be suitable. Other entertainments might include a mathematics trail around the school, or competitions. Even such old favourites as guessing the number of sweets in a jar or the weight of a cake have a mathematical basis!

A teacher or teachers should be available to explain how and why games are used in the classroom, and to give advice to any parent who may want to undertake similar activities at home. It might be useful to have a display of books and a leaflet prepared to suggest further activities for parents to try.

If you prefer cooperation to competition, parents and children alike could be invited to construct small tetrahedrons to help stellate an icosahedron;

to continue a pattern using ideas of symmetry; or just to watch a film strip such as *Donald Duck in Mathemagic Land* together.

Whatever events are included in the games and entertainment room the emphasis should be on mathematics, for parents and children alike, as an enjoyable activity and not a stressful one. The pupils organising the games need to be prepared to encourage both young children and diffident parents in their attempts. Although many children are experts at cajoling family members into joining in their games, it might be as well to offer them a little further training with other pupils or members of staff before the event takes place.

How it Worked:

MATHS THROUGH FUN AND GAMES

Last February we helped with the maths evening. It was a big success. We were doing tetrahedrons with compasses and rulers. We made ten. It was hard to get parents to join in because they did not feel like doing something so long. Then we went and did a Tables Tournament. We took it in turns to play against the parents. Lots of people had a go and others watched. One Chinese man liked the Tables Tournament that much he said he was going to take the idea of the game back to his country!

Nicholas Milsom, Sarah Witty and **Simon Baxter** (aged 10)

Games to play

10 Parents Working with Groups of Pupils

Scope

- Can happen as part of the ordinary school day or during extracurricular activities.

- More usually a feature of nursery and primary schools. (Even in schools where there is already a tradition of this type of parental involvement, it may be necessary to bring out the mathematical nature of the work undertaken.)

- Could be introduced as a follow up to other forms of parental involvement e.g. observing lessons, accompanying outings, etc.

ADVANTAGES	DISADVANTAGES
Can strengthen links between the community and the school.	*Requires long term commitment from parents.*
Parents may gain understanding of what the school is striving to achieve and the teachers' role in this.	*Requires both time and sensitivity from the teacher organising the working groups.*
Pupils benefit from discussing their findings within a structured group.	*May require alteration in other classroom activities to accommodate the groups.*
	Some restrictions may be imposed by LEA's, unions, insurance, etc.

In many primary schools parents are invited to share their talents and their time by working with small groups of children within the school. In such a school, one parent might be found telling stories in the reading corner; another talking to children as they experiment with sand and water; a third helping a small group to do some baking and a fourth displaying newly finished work. Parents, pupils and teachers stand to benefit from the increased communication such involvement can bring.

The range of abilities and interests offered by each parent varies considerably. Skill and diplomacy are needed by the teacher who is to assess and use these in the most effective way! The chosen activity must be thoroughly discussed with each helper beforehand so that he or she is aware of the aims of the work. (This is perhaps particularly important when the activity is of a mathematical nature: not every volunteer will immediately appreciate the significance of estimating weights when baking, or the relevance of sorting activities.) Discussion between the teacher and the helper after the event is important too, since the teacher needs to know how the activity has progressed and the problems and achievements experienced by both the parent and the pupils.

How it Worked:

i A PARENT IN AN INFANT CLASSROOM

I approached the Head and requested that I might become a volunteer helper in the Infants' class on Friday mornings. I was particularly interested in what the children did in a normal working day since my daughter had started her education in a very different school.

During the first term I helped small groups of children to discuss pictures which involved basic counting and sets. I enjoyed this and the children found it helpful to relate numbers to everyday situations.

Later all our attention was directed to the new computer. My job was to assist the children in learning the layout of the computer and to rectify errors when the wrong button was pushed. Children did basic counting – trains flashed up and they had to key in the correct number. The slightly older children used a program which required speed and visual capabilities in order to specify how many dots had flashed up in a given time. I found that this work, though initially exciting for the children, soon became very boring. Children who experienced failure tended to become negative in their attitude towards the computer. Others, I felt, expressed a desire to move forward but the program did not cater for this.

As an observer in the classroom, it is very easy to be critical when you are not actually doing the teaching! I felt that the children enjoyed my visits and it broadened their experiences to work with an adult other than their teacher. I intend to offer my services again as soon as my baby is at play-school and I have a free morning again.

Ms Diana Nicholson

ii A SURVEY OF TWO SCHOOLS

In the primary school, children are acquiring a range of skills and experiencing a variety of methods of learning. They are learning to think and to discover. Discussion between adult and pupil and between one pupil and another is essential, as is a great deal of practical work. Much of this takes place in small groups and many primary teachers welcome extra help from volunteers (usually mothers) in these activities.

In an effort to find out, on a very small scale, what everyone concerned felt, a small study involving two schools was set up. Both schools were first schools with about 170 pupils, but serving very different catchment areas. Questionnaires were sent to every parent and elicited a high level of response. A sample of parents was also selected to follow up this questionnaire by an open-ended, semi-structured interview. Staff and children were also interviewed (although interviewing is not altogether a suitable technique with very young children).

On analysing the responses, it appeared that parents were generally very happy to be involved in the less academic aspects of school life, such as school trips, cooking, helping with art and craft or changing at the swimming baths. They were not so happy about helping in areas such as listening to children read or playing mathematical games. These areas were felt to be a job for the professionals. The parents who actually did help in school often felt that they would like more advice and guidance in what they were doing.

One parent said 'My respect for the teachers has increased enormously . . . just seeing how they handle the situation – and all those instructions!' However, perhaps the last word should come from a child: when asked if it was a good idea to have parents as helpers in the class, one replied 'Yes . . . because you can get learnt a bit more quicker!'

P Dawson (Westfield County Primary School, Haverhill, Suffolk)

Parents at work with small groups

11 Mathematics Taken out of Schools

Scope

- Seeks to involve the whole community in a greater appreciation of the role of mathematics.

ADVANTAGES	DISADVANTAGES
Strengthens links between home and school.	*Requires long term commitment from all those involved.*
Increases discussion of mathematics between parents, teachers and pupils.	*Can be very time-consuming.*
Increases the prestige of mathematics in the school.	*Needs a great deal of imaginative organisation.*

The aim of this approach is to influence the attitudes towards mathematics of the whole community served by the school. Parents and children undertake a variety of activities designed to draw mathematics out of the world around them. Parents are not expected to *teach* their children mathematics, but to *learn* from them and alongside them.

Such a scheme is clearly a long-term venture and could be developed over a term, a year, or even longer. To keep up the momentum, a number of different topics will be needed and a range of styles of presentation can be employed. Indeed a project such as this could incorporate any, or all, of the events already outlined in this book. (The emphasis of each event would need to be changed so that the mathematics presented could be undertaken as a family activity.)

A possible programme of events might include:

1 A *talk* to set the scene.

2 A *workshop* session based on the first topic to be covered. Each family attending would be given a follow-up pack of activities and equipment in order to pursue the topic further at home.

43

3 A weekly *open lesson* in school. Pupils would be working on the topic in hand. Parents could work with their own children, or by themselves, or observe all the activities in progress.

This pattern could be repeated every half term with a new topic. However, additional events might also be included to support and extend this programme. For example:

1 A *stall* in school selling mathematical books, games and puzzles.

2 A *games and entertainments* room so that parents with younger children are not excluded from the school-based sessions.

3 A *display* of work generated by the topic and of the resources used.

4 A *telephone help-line* to encourage parents stuck on their 'homework'.

5 Further mathematical activities organised outside school hours and open to parents and children alike, e.g. a computer club, a Saturday morning circus or a mathematical trail around the locality. (Such activities could also be used to recruit new volunteers for the next series of sessions.)

A few tips:
- Try a mini-project first in order to assess the response of parents, pupils and teachers and to streamline your organisation for a full-scale project.

- Recruit outside experts to help to compile the packs of resources as well as to organise individual sessions. Mathematics advisers, advisory teachers, teachers in other schools and the parents themselves may all be able to help.

- Remember to invite prospective parents too.

- Regularly review the impact of the project and the progress being made.

How it Worked:

i THE STUTTON PROJECT

Here at Stutton, we have been operating a home-reading partnership scheme for some time. The clear gains this caused in both attitude and understanding raised another question: why not try a similar venture for mathematics?

It wasn't difficult to organise our maths project once we were clear about why we were doing it, what we hoped to achieve and how. (A lot of talking was needed to clear this stage out of the way, but to go ahead without the full commitment and agreement of everyone involved would have been asking for trouble.) In placing adults alongside their children as participants in the activities, rather than allowing them any supervisory or corrective role, it was hoped to alter both the children's and the parents' attitude to mathematics to a more positive and enthusiastic one. This also coincides with the preferred mode of teaching of the staff generally.

The next step was to produce the first unit booklet. We chose metric measurement as our topic. This involved a lot of extra secretarial and reprographic time, but was straightforward. Once this was done, we were ready to present it to the parents. We needed to explain to them that it was an experimental project, and that we were not trying to teach them to teach their children maths, give extra homework or anything like that. In many ways this was the hardest thing to get across and has had to be repeated many times.

The response was good. This is a small village school and, of our 41 families, 30 families became involved in the scheme. The first meeting was for adults, but on the second evening the whole familes were invited. All the nine activities in the unit booklet were set up in the hall and the adults could watch the children at work, lend a hand or try out the activities themselves. No one had time to do more than two of the activities, but they went away with the booklets having seen all the activities in action. Some six weeks were allowed to complete this unit. All the activities were practical and really needed no recording, although some families produced elaborate charts, graphs and so on. Materials and equipment, such as measuring tapes, metre sticks, stopwatches, gridsheets etc., were loaned out by the school as required.

Throughout the six-week period, Friday mornings in school were given over to the activities in the booklet and were open to parents. Many parents were disappointed not to be able to attend these sessions, which became interesting social events, but those who could quickly became regulars. One bonus of these sessions was that, with large numbers of people working on mathematical tasks, the enthusiasm was catching. Things often came to a stop while we all went to see why excited noises were coming from the group in the corner timing toy cars down a series of ramps, or from the group swinging pendulums from the PE apparatus! The nature of these in-school sessions changed during the term. The first couple were like the original workshop. The hall was set up with two or three activities and parents would collect their children from class and work in the hall with a teacher. This gave them the opportunity to see some of the activities explored in more depth than was likely at home. Later some parents expressed the desire to see this sort of work in a classroom setting and offered to help. So the next sessions were arranged in class. Parents sat amongst the children, listened to the teacher's introduction, then everyone got on with it. This was the most demanding session for the teachers involved – and the least enjoyed by the children!

At about this time, it was felt that a systematic effort should be made to involve those children whose families were not participating in the project at home. The final couple of sessions reverted to the hall-activity-circus format, but with the parent regulars now working with and alongside other people's children. Interestingly, this was the part of the project most enjoyed by parents and many felt that they had gained more insight from this than from anything else.

Many families found that the children's enthusiasm displayed at the evening workshop and Friday morning sessions, had disappeared when the parents suggested doing another activity from the booklet at home. This did not surprise us, or dismay us, but it may be that we will run more school-based events and try to offer even more support next time. We will certainly try to link the mathematical content of the next unit even more closely with real life and employ an investigative approach wherever possible. Most encouragingly, we feel that we shall be engaged in a meaningful way with our parents, in pursuit of the kind of powerful partnership which we are sure could improve mathematical education.

Laurie Rousham (Stutton CE County Primary School, Ipswich)

ii QUICK TIP MATHS

Quick Tipmaths

mums and dads are usually better than us kids but sometimes us kids are better than mums and dads. Soon friday mums and Dads were allowed to come to school to learn some more about maths. Things like cubic shape that means funny shape building bricks and lengh. money is another one. my mum and Dad got on well.

Simon (aged 7)

iii SUPER MATHS

Super Maths

My mum came to maths on friday and we made a giant that was six cubits and three hand spans long when we went to maths in the evening. I liked racing cars and using the stop watches best. I liked making the pendulums as well Anthony had the biggest hand span. I didn't work with my mum becase she was mesurcring string

(Simon aged 8)

iv A PARENT REPLIES

As a parent I looked forward to the chance of working with my children on a maths project. With the introduction of the home-reading scheme, I had seen their development in reading and English as they had come up through the school, but their maths was still a bit of an unknown to me. I did not entirely understand their books, which use different methods and signs to my own, so their progress was difficult to follow. I would also have the chance to find out about the philosophy of modern maths. Both the evening and the morning sessions lived up to my expectations and I thoroughly enjoyed working with my children, finding it much easier than trying to do things at home. They behaved maturely and responsibly and we learned a lot from each other. It was interesting to see their ability for working things out for themselves, but it was hard not to tell them the answers – parents need educating too! Parents certainly need to trust and believe in both the teacher and the methods used, otherwise their presence can only be bad for themselves and the child. Some parents found it difficult to maintain the concentration of their children: it might be beneficial to move the children round so that they work with different adults. The main impression I had was how much the children enjoyed these sessions – even those who find maths hard – and how different it all was from my own school experiences. There was a point to everything we did and the children learnt from a living situation instead of a piece of paper. I feel convinced that maths taught in this way will give children confidence and understanding of the subject and how to use it, and as the project continues my own knowledge and awareness of my children's maths increases.

Mrs Terry Drane

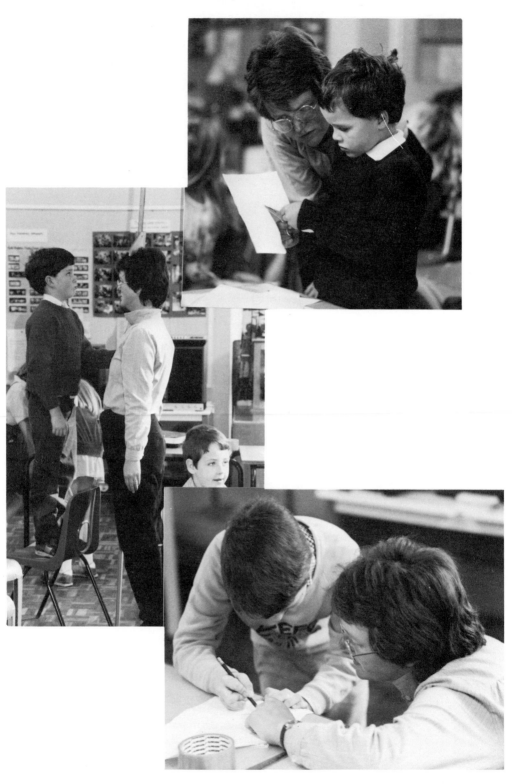

Find an adult and measure carefully

SECTION 2 Resources

The resources in this section have all been used successfully in mathematical events. They give some idea of the range of possibilities, but are not intended as models. What is appropriate for any particular school depends on the mathematics curriculum and the general philosophy of the school as much as on the type of event planned.

12   Letters to Parents

> **The first thing to do is to send an invitation.**
> **Here are some sample letters.**

a

Dear Parents,

On 4th February from 6 p.m. to 8.30 p.m., you are invited to visit the school when there will be an opportunity to see groups of children involved in a variety of activities. This will be a different kind of open night from those previously held. The teachers obviously will be supervising their groups of children and it will not be possible for them to answer questions about an individual's progress, problems, etc. I plan to hold the more traditional type of open night later in the year after school reports have been issued. Nearer 4th February, I shall be asking permission for your children to attend school during that evening.

I do not know how many parents will be attending and should be grateful if you would complete and return the detachable form below.

All good wishes for the New Year.

Yours sincerely,

. . . .

. . . .

I/We do/do not intend to visit the school during the evening of Monday, 4th February.

Name . . . .

Parent/guardian of . . . . in class . . . .

51

b

Dear Parent,

Now that the children have settled into the routine of school, I am writing to extend an invitation to anyone who would like to be a voluntary helper in the classroom.

There are many ways in which parents can help in the classroom by working with small groups in art/craft activities:
talking about model making;
talking about sand and water play;
use of educational games, etc.

If you have an hour or so to spare each week, either morning or afternoon, please pop in and see Mr . . . . or me. I'm sorry however that I cannot accommodate pre-school children.

Yours sincerely,

. . . .
Headmistress

c

Dear Parents,

How often have you wondered what your children are doing in maths these days? On Monday, 28th February, from 7.30 p.m. to 9 p.m. you are invited to come and see. There will be an extensive display of children's work and a description and explanation of the various aspects of mathematics studied in all years. A local toyshop is providing a selection of mathematical games, books and puzzles which can be ordered through the school.

Tea will be available during the evening and a 'Beetle Drive' and other games will be organised for children who want to join in.

Yours sincerely,

. . . .
Head of Mathematics

d

Dear Parent,

A great deal of change has taken place recently in the teaching of mathematics and we should very much like you to see the type of teaching and learning experience that your child has in this subject at this school.

DATE: THURSDAY, 19TH NOVEMBER

TIME: 7.30-8.45 p.m.

PLACE: MATHEMATICS ROOMS and the HALL OF LOWER SCHOOL.

Please enter school by way of the LOWER SCHOOL FOYER.

There will be an opportunity for you to see children at work and indeed to participate yourself. Refreshments will be served by the Parents' Association. I hope that you will be able to attend and look forward to meeting you.

I should be grateful if you would complete and return the reply slip to your child's mathematics teacher by Monday, 16th November.

Yours sincerely,

. . . .

Headmaster

REPLY SLIP

To: The Headmaster

MATHEMATICS   THURSDAY
EVENING   19th NOVEMBER

I will/will not be able to attend and I wish to reserve . . . . . . places for the mathematics evening.

Signed . . . . Parent/Guardian

Pupil's name . . . . Form . . . .

Please return this slip to your son's/daughter's MATHEMATICS teacher by MONDAY, 16th NOVEMBER.

13   Activities for Parents on Arrival

i GRAPHS

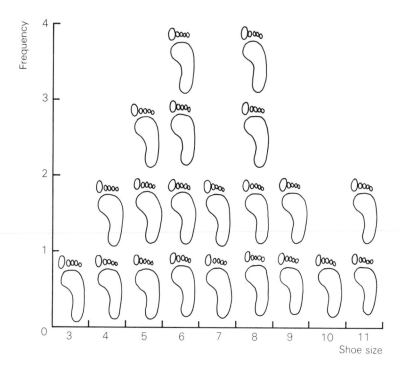

A graph of parents' shoe sizes

Graphs are not the only kind of
mathematical picture.
Here are two more introductory
activities for parents on arrival.
Both use mathematical pictures.

ii FLOW CHARTS

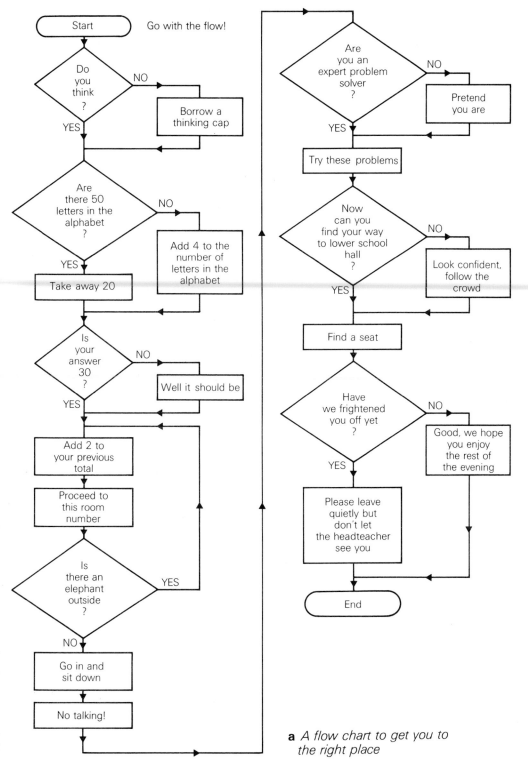

a A flow chart to get you to the right place

iii VENN DIAGRAMS

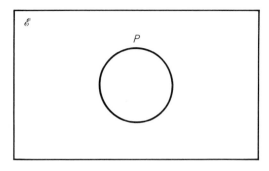

$\mathscr{E}$ is the set of people attending the opening evening.

P is the set of people with at least one child at the school.

Where do you belong?

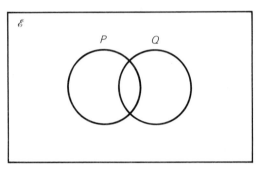

Q is the set of people who enjoy maths.

Where do you belong?

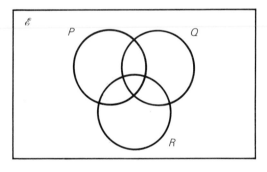

R is the set of people who think they are good at maths.

Where do you belong?

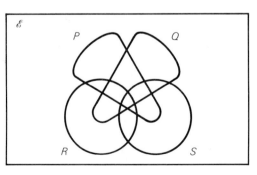

S is the set of people who think they can put their flag in the right place.

Where do you belong?

Put your flag in the last diagram.

b *Venn diagrams to show where you belong*

56

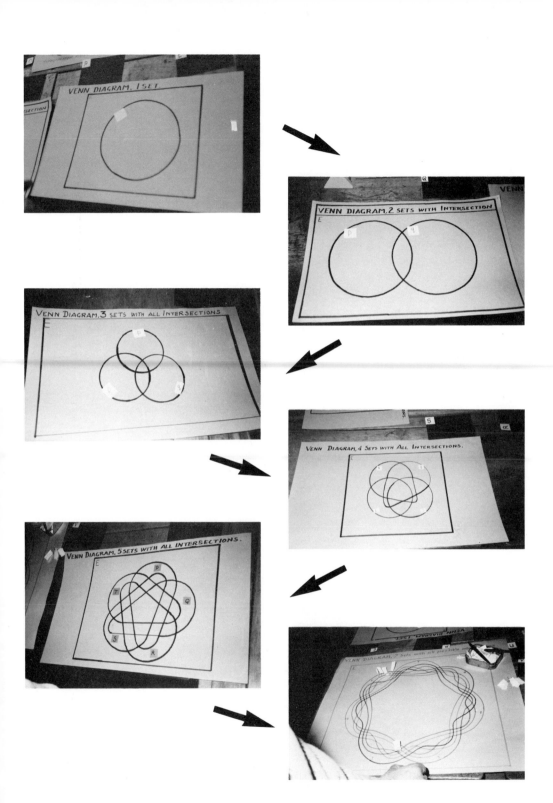

These photographs were taken near the start of this activity for parents at a middle school

14 Some Activities for Groups of Parents

i SORTING – A TEACHER-LED ACTIVITY

Many primary schools start their work in mathematics by giving children sorting experiences which subsequently lead on to number work. There may be some parents who do not understand the rationale behind this experience and feel that their children are merely playing rather than undertaking a genuine mathematical activity.

A variety of sorting activities for parents can be organised using attribute blocks, pictures and 'odds and ends'. The teacher might begin with a demonstration emphasising appropriate vocabulary and follow this with a workshop in which parents sort and re-sort the apparatus themselves and discuss their results. Discussion of what happens with four, five or even seven intersecting sets is possible (see the photographs on page 57). Children's work can be used to illustrate the use of sorting and matching activities in later number work.

ii COORDINATES – A TEACHER-LED ACTIVITY

The following activity is just one way of introducing coordinates which can help to link the concept to ordered pairs used in life outside the classroom.

1 Arrange the room so that the parents sit in groups around tables.

2 Start with a preliminary discussion of hotel room numbers. Why are room numbers such as 116 or 302 common in even quite small hotels?

3 Give out a numbered card to each table. Give another numbered card to each person at each table, using 1, 2, 3 for a table with three people and 1, 2, 3, 4, 5 for a table with five people, etc.

4 Discuss how these numbers can be used to give everyone in the room a unique number.

5 Ask all the parents to say their own number and record it on the board, e.g. (3, 2) for the second person at the third table.

6 Discuss the link between (3, 2) and (5, 2) as well as that between (3, 2) and (3, 3) etc.

7 Further discussion could then be used to consider alternative ways of ordering the numbers now displayed on the board; other possible uses of an ordered pair system and even other ways of designating each person in the room uniquely.

iii SOME SIMPLER ACTIVITIES THAT PUPILS COULD LEAD

a GRAPHS

Collection of statistical information collated by pupils and displayed before the parents leave. Examples: birthday month, eye colour, initial letter of first name, etc.

b JUST A MINUTE

Can you judge a minute?

This needs a stopwatch which can be handled by a child. Parents are then asked to indicate when they think a minute has passed. The results could be displayed graphically and prizes awarded for accuracy.

c TIME PASSES

When was a million seconds ago?

A discussion topic: calculators might be useful.

d MUCH ADO ABOUT NOTHING

What is special about zero (nought)?

This could be given as a 'quiet' activity and followed by a pooling of ideas.

e TERRIBLE TABLES TESTS

See p. 60

f SPIDERS

See p. 60

Terrible Tables Test

Prepare worksheets in advance with randomly selected numbers at the beginning of each row and column.

Competitors, in pairs or in a larger group, have to complete the table as quickly as possible. The winner is the person who completes the table correctly in the shortest time. Incorrect entries may either be discarded or given penalty points for each error.

×	0	5	9	6	3	1	8	4	7	10
2										
9										
7										
4										
3										
5										
12										
8										
6										
11										

Spiders

Someone suggests a starting number and everyone supplies a fact about it which is entered in a radial form.

The idea is that patterns should be noted and used to generate more and more mathematical facts.

This activity can also be made competitive by asking individuals to enter as many facts as possible in a limited time.

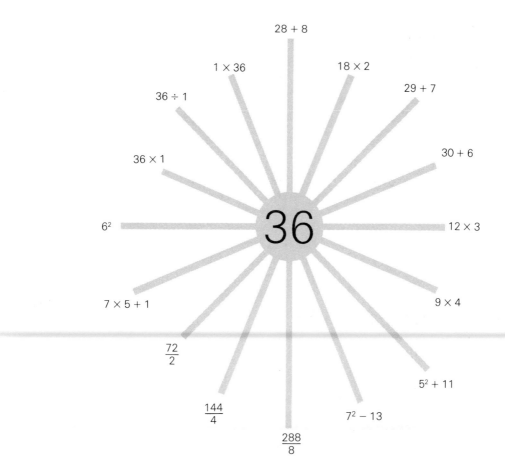

15 Worksheet Ideas

It can be useful to have prepared worksheets
so that parents can get involved in mathematical activity.
Here are some examples:
the first set (i–iv)
is ready for immediate use.
The second (v–ix)
may require preparation and/or equipment.

Quick, Easily Produced Materials

i

Aim

To test powers of comprehension and logical perception.

Method

Study the following:

> Smith, Jones, Brown, (John, Peter and David) are three teachers at Glenbank School, teaching different subjects. Smith teaches French, Brown gives the science teacher a lift home in his car, John teaches art and David cannot stand the smell of the Chemistry laboratories.

Match the first and second names of each teacher.

ii

Aim

To give practice in square numbers and square roots. (Any number of players.)

Materials

Ordinary pack of cards with the jacks, queens and kings taken out. Aces count as 1.

Method

Each player is dealt five cards. Starting with the player on the dealer's left, they take it in turns to play a card. After each play, a new card is given so the players always have five cards.

As each card is played, the total of all cards played so far is kept. When the total reaches a square number, the player of the last card scores the square root of the number. Play stops when the total reaches or passes 200. The winner is the player who scores most points.

For the confused here is an example:

Alan plays   4   total   4   Alan scores 2
Bella plays   5   total   9   Bella scores 3
Chris plays   9   total 18
Alan plays 10   total 28
Bella plays   8   total 36   Bella scores 6

iii

Aim

To examine ability in extracting information from a diagram.

Method

Study the following:

Bus timetable

DEPART		ARRIVE	
Little Hampton	07 00	Hampton	07 10
Hampton	07 15	Big Hampton	07 25
Big Hampton	07 30	Ambridge	07 45
Ambridge	07 50	Dale	08 10
Dale	08 12	Down	08 35
Down	08 40	Fineton	08 50

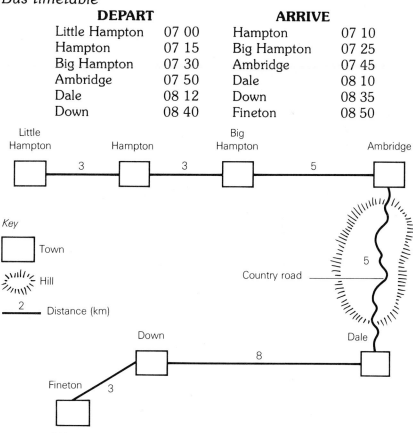

A plan of the route

63

a Is it a morning or evening bus?

b How long will the bus from Little Hampton take to reach:
  1 Big Hampton?
  2 Dale?

c How long does the bus wait at:
  1 Ambridge?
  2 Dale?

d How long does the journey from Little Hampton to Fineton take?

e What makes the journey slower between Ambridge and Dale?

f How far is it from:
  1 Little Hampton to Ambridge?
  2 Big Hampton to Fineton?

iv

Aim

To provide a simple exercise in basic number awareness.

Materials

Paper and pencil.

Method

Take turns to use *one* of the numbers 0, 1, 2, 3, 4, 5, 6, 7, 8 or 9.

You must not use the same number twice.

To win make a line add up to 10.

Here is an example:

Step 1

| | 5 | |

Step 2

| | 5 | |
| 7 | | |

Step 3

| | 5 | 6 |
| 7 | | |

Step 4

| | 5 | 6 |
| 7 | | 0 |

Step 5

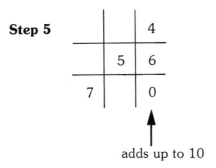

adds up to 10

Materials Needing Preparation and/or Equipment

v

Aim

To become familiar with the litre.

To have some idea of how much liquid makes up a litre.

Materials

Litre container

Cup

Water

Variety of containers smaller than the litre container.

Method

Find out how many cups of water will be needed to fill the litre container. Have a guess before you try. Record like this:

Guess	cups
Actual	cups

How near were you?

Now try estimating with other containers which you have, e.g. bottle, tin, jar, etc.

Record like this:

No. of times to fill	CONTAINERS					
	cup	mug	jar	tin	bowl	thimble
Guess						
Actual						

vi

Aim

To provide an interesting follow-up activity to work involving line symmetry.

Materials

Small mirror or reflective perspex, pencil.

Method

Sixteen letters of the alphabet have been cut in half along an axis of symmetry and stuck together in pairs. Can you find out which ones they are? Use your mirror to help you. The first one is done for you.

Line symmetry

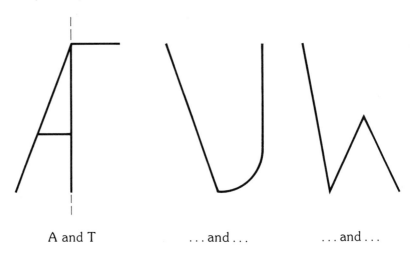

A and T   . . . and . . .   . . . and . . .

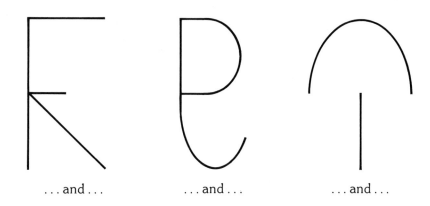

...and...   ...and...   ...and...

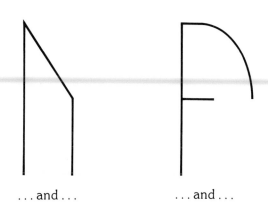

...and...   ...and...

vii

Aim

To give practical application to the terms tessellation and symmetry.
To develop the skills of folding and sticking.

Materials

Card

Pencil

Scissors

Glue

Ruler

Clip

Method

Cut out 12 pieces of card the size of this template:

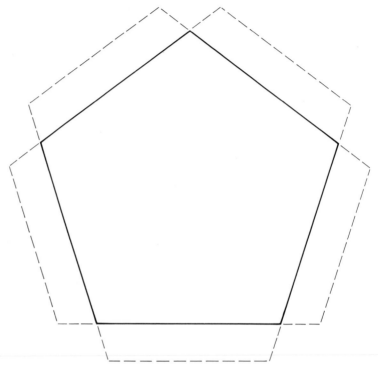

The template

Score along the lines and fold back the flaps.

Stick five of the pentagons, one to each edge of a sixth.

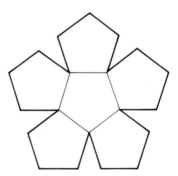

Half of a dodecahedron

Fold the five pentagons back and stick them to each other.

Repeat the procedure with the six remaining pentagons.

Glue the two halves of the dodecahedron together, two or three tabs at a time.

Aim

To show that, for a right-angled triangle, the area of the square on the longest side (hypotenuse) is equal to the total area formed by the squares on the other two sides.

Materials

A large piece of card with the following diagram on:

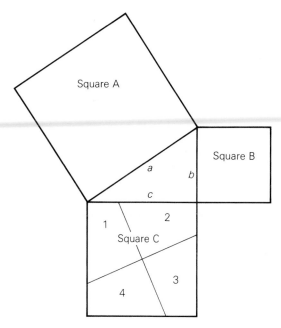

Three squares on a triangle

Five pieces of card cut into exactly the same shape and size as the areas marked Square B, 1, 2, 3, 4.

Method

Try to fit the five shapes labelled Square B, 1, 2, 3, 4 into the large square A. When you have done so you have demonstrated Pythagoras's formula for right-angled triangles.

The formula can be derived as follows:

Area of Square A = Area of Square B + Area of Square C

$$a \times a \quad = \quad b \times b \quad + \quad c \times c$$

$$a^2 \quad = \quad b^2 \quad + \quad c^2$$

Aim

To practise using a calculator and to demonstrate that no machine can produce the required answers until the operator has worked out what to do!

Materials

Calculators and crossword sheets.

Calculator crossword

Some numbers on the calculator spell words, if you turn the calculator round to read them. The answers to this crossword are all words but the clues give you the numbers to make them.

Clues across

1 The creatures in 6 across may be sore but at least they are not 5 million more than 537 637.

4 Just $\frac{1}{2}$.

6 400 millipedes have lost 20 096 legs. What must they do on those they have left?

8 $11 + (6^2 \times 157)$ of these should not be put in one basket.

9 $7 + 8^2$. Watch out, it is French!

10 $75^2 + 45^2 + 8^2$ is a lump of ground.

11 Look at all those people: 5 regiments each with 27 companies of 269 soldiers. What's happening?

12 37 hundredths is a lion of a number.

Clues down

2 20% of 1 883 080 is no laughing matter.

3 David ate 5 sweets and gave 40 to each of his 20 friends. Now he has none left, what does he do?

4 Once upon a time Miss Muffett bought 221 shares for £1 each. Now they are each worth £36. What does the profit tell her to do?

5 By mistake the school ordered 7 boxes each containing 7 packets of 113 sheets of blotting paper. Look at what arrived and say what was wanted.

7 Jack and who climbed 10 across? Add 4 to that answer to find out.

10 Who's $2^5 + 2$? The cat's grandfather?

Now make up some of your own clues.

16 Problems for More Confident Parents

Try Them Yourself First!

i The different magic square

1	2	3	4
5	6	7	8
9	10	11	12
13	14	15	16

Ring any number.

Cross out all the figures in the same row and column.

Ring any other number not crossed out.

Cross out all numbers in the same row and column.

Repeat.

Now ring the remaining number.

Find the total of the numbers ringed.

What do you notice?

Can you explain the result?

ii Squared

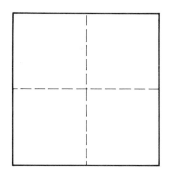

Draw a square.

Divide this square into four squares.

Try to make 5, 7, 10, 12, 8 squares.

Could you make 97, 54 squares for example?

What numbers of squares is it impossible to make?

Note: The squares need not be the same size.

iii 1001

Write down any three numbers.

Repeat them so that you have a six-digit number.

Divide this number by 7.

71

Are there any remainders?

Divide the answer by 11.

Are there remainders?

Divide the answer by 13.

Explain your result.

iv Pentominoes

A pentomino is made by drawing five squares so that adjacent sides coincide.

e.g.

How many different pentominoes can you find?

Try it for three squares, four squares, etc. Is there a pattern in the numbers that can be made?

v Handshakes

There are a certain number of people at a party.

Each person shakes hands exactly once with each other person present.

There were 28 handshakes altogether.

How many people were there at the party?

vi Lockers

At the closing ceremony of an American graduate group, all 100 graduates stand in front of their lockers.

When the signal is given the first student opens all the locker doors.

The second student follows and closes the second and every second locker in the row.

The third student changes the state of the third and every third locker and this continues through to the hundredth student.

Which locker doors were open at the end and why?

(Who said mathematics was sensible – only the committed will want to try this useless exercise!)

Hints

It would take the fun out of it to give the solutions, but here are some indications of the mathematics involved. If you need some help you may find it here.

What is a triangular number?

Look for number factors.

There are 1, 1, 2, 5, 12 ...

You can always make four squares from one square.

Multiplication by 10, 100, 1000, in a place value system.

How many factors has each of the following numbers?
7, 12, 25

If you can make five squares you can make any multiple of a certain number more than five.

You only use one number from each row and each column.

The pattern in rows is increasing by one, in columns by a different number.

Multiplication by 1 can be expressed in many different ways.

17

Miscellaneous Resources

i IN-SERVICE WORK ON PARENTAL INVOLVEMENT

Communicating with Parents

SMP In-service Resource Kit, CUP

This kit consists of an A4 wallet containing leader's notes and a battery of resources including: acetate sheets of statements on communicating with parents; letters and report forms from various schools; a slide and tape sequence on mathematics as it is taught today; and even a pack of 'chance' cards indicating possible comments from parents about the mathematics in school. It is aimed at the mathematics department of any secondary school that wishes to review the manner in which parents are informed of both the work of the department and the progress of their children within it. The worksheets encourage teachers to ask themselves some very pertinent questions such as 'Exactly what information would parents receive about maths and their child during his/her career at this school?' The emphasis is on a review of present practice. What might constitute *good* practice is left to the imagination and vision of the teachers involved.

Mathematics for Parents of Young Children

E Choat and P Kivotos, EFVA, Paxton Place, Gypsy Road, London SE27

Nine 20-minute videos show infants, and occasionally older children, at work in school. Their activities of painting, story telling, playing at trains, etc. are put into a mathematical context. The teacher explains the value of the activities and discusses with parents similar activities that they could undertake at home. The handbook which accompanies the series gives a synopsis of each tape, expands on the follow-up activities, and lists some ideas parents might try to draw out of them. Activities suitable for workshop sessions with parents are also outlined.

IMPACT (ILEA Mathematics for Parents, Children and Teachers)

Department of Teaching Studies, Polytechnic of North London, Prince of Wales Road, London NW5

This scheme has been piloted in nine primary schools with teachers and lecturers producing games and investigations for family use. As a result a starter pack of 50 activities is now available. A further three-year research project is now being undertaken in Oxfordshire and the London Borough of Barnet. One of the outcomes of this will be the development of materials to support in-service work on initiating parental involvement in mathematics.

ii BOOKLETS SUPPORTING PARENTAL INVOLVEMENT IN MATHEMATICS

More and more Local Education Authorities are publishing booklets for parents about the provision of primary education in the area. Most of these are general accounts covering all aspects of school life, only a few specialise in mathematics,

e.g. *Mathematics in Suffolk Schools*
Primary Mathematics and Parents (Hertfordshire)

Since 1979 there has been a parents' booklet published in the *Mathematics for Schools* series. It is a small book which carefully describes the structure and methodology of the mathematics scheme. Few other publishers have thought it necessary to produce similar explanatory guides for parents. However, recently Ginn has produced a *Parents' Guide*. This small pamphlet aims to describe primary school mathematics today and ways parents can help their young children through mathematical activities at home, as well as to introduce the Ginn mathematics scheme. It could be useful in any primary school.

iii ADDITIONAL RESOURCES FOR MATHEMATICAL WORKSHOPS

The number of books of problems, investigations and games is increasing all the time. You will have your favourite ones no doubt, but when you are planning a mathematical event for whole families you may need to increase the range of activities you offer. Listed here are a number of sources of excellent materials for mathematical diversions to suit all tastes and budgets!

The Association of Teachers of Mathematics

7 Shaftesbury Street, Derby DE3 8YB

An increasing number of items is for sale,

e.g. *Away With Maths* (materials for a mathematical weekend)
Mathematical Activity Tiles (for 3D constructions)
Points of Departure (investigations)
Polyhedra (posters and postcards)
'L' A Mathemagical Adventure Program

Birmingham Mathematics Resource Centre

Ada Road, Birmingham BB9 4NG

Teachers at this centre have produced a pack of calculator workcards and a pack of multicultural maths activities.

Cranfield Press

Cranfield Institute of Technology, Management Library,
Cranfield, Bedford MK43 0AL

This press publishes the early books by the Spode Group on using mathematics to solve real problems.

Eigen Publications

39 Den Bank Crescent, Sheffield, S10 5PB

Dave Kirby, Des Wilson and others are producing a steady stream of booklets of investigations and games for primary children and infants,
e.g.   *Investigation Bank* (20 booklets)
  Mathematics in Sport (7 booklets)
  Maths Games in the Classroom (22 booklets)
  Shape Activities (11 booklets)

Excitement in Learning

88 Mint Street, London SE1 1QX

This company sells an incredible range of gridsheets and also produce LEAP. This is an acronym for Local Educational Authority Publications. It does not in fact list all the LEA publications, but it is still a useful resource.

Hodge Hill School

Bromford Road, Hodge Hill, Birmingham

Puzzle cards and booklets of ideas written by Geoff Fowler and other teachers are sold in aid of school funds,
e.g.   *Activity-pax*
  Investi-pax
  Maths-pax

Keele Mathematical Educational Publications

F. R. Watson, Department of Education, University of Keele,
Staffs ST5 5BG

F. R. Watson and others produce interesting investigations and calculator booklets, but possibly of even more value is the ITeMS Catalogue in which any group producing Ideas in the Teaching of Mathematics and Science may advertise.

ILEA

Despatch Centre, Centre for Learning Resources,
275 Kennington Lane, London SE11 5QZ

ILEA has recently published a pack of mathematical games called 'Count Me In', with engaging multi-ethnic illustrations.

The Longfield Press

6 Longfield Gardens, Tring, Hertfordshire HP23 4DN

Alan Parr specialises in tiny booklets full of exciting mathematical games,
e.g. *Acorns*
Entertain
It's Magic
25 Mathematical Card Games
Pick a Pair
Playground/Groundplay
Tournament

Manchester Maths Resource Group

Polytechnic School of Education, 799 Wilmslow Road,
Manchester M20 8RR

Gillian Hatch has collected lots of ideas for mathematical investigations,
e.g. *Bounce To It* (infants)
Calculator Workshop (primary)
Jump To It (primary and lower secondary)
Leap To It (primary and lower secondary)
Puzzle Cards (primary)
Shape Workshop

The Mathematical Association

259 London Road, Leicester LE2 3BE

Classroom resources, as well as books like this, are produced by members
of the Mathematical Association,
e.g. *Calculator Activity Sheets*
Posters and Puzzle Postcards
Pull Apart Tangram Squares
132 Short Programs

The National Association for Remedial Education

2 Lichfield Road, Stafford ST17 4JX

Although NARE produces more materials for remedial language work,
some mathematical materials are produced too,
e.g. *Number Activities and Games*

Normac Publications

Barry Pinfield, Charlestown Primary School, Pilkington Road,
Blackley, Manchester M9 2BH

The Northern Region Mathematics Centre has amongst its publications
some books of games,
e.g. *More Number Games*
Number Fun
Practical Number Games

Resources for Learning Development Unit

Bishop Road, Bishopton, Bristol, BS7 8LS

A wide variety of topic packs and other stimulating classroom materials including worksheets, games and software are produced.

The Shell Centre for Mathematical Education

University of Nottingham, Nottingham NG7 2RD

Recent materials from this group include resources for extended investigations for secondary school pupils, software and videos,

e.g. *Be a Paper Engineer*
Design a Board Game
Problems with Patterns and Numbers
Run a Quiz

The Slide Centre Ltd

Ilton, Ilminster, Somerset

A large selection of slides and filmstrips on mathematical topics is available.

Tarquin Publications

Stradbroke, Diss IP21 5JP

This must be one of the best collections of classroom resources for practical mathematics and they are all beautifully produced,

e.g. *Make Shapes 1, 2, 3*
Mathematical Curiosities 1, 2, 3
Mirror Puzzles
Polysymmetrics
Posters and Postcards